AND WE MET AGAIN

(Story of Rudra and Shaivi)

SHIVANI SINGH

PAPER TOWNS
PUBLISHERS

PAPER TOWNS
PUBLISHERS

First published by

Papertowns Publishers
72, Vishwanath Dham Colony,
Niwaru Road, Jhotwara,
Jaipur, 302012

And We Met Again (Story of Rudra and Shaivi)

ISBN Print Book – 978-93-6185-429-3

Printed in India

About the one who read eyes,

to those who read books.

PREFACE

I thought we were one flame—

dancing, daring, undoing everything

that distance had built...

until I saw his eyes.

ACKNOWLEDGEMENT

This book is a testament to the fact that even in the deepest sorrow, love sustains.

I began writing this manuscript just to have an anchor during the long hours of vigil in the ICU, sitting by my grandmother's side. It was only later I realized that those collected pages formed a complete book. The collection was unintended which turned out to be a surprising solace which was completed in her loving presence. I know that if she were still here, she would be the only person most proud of this debut. This book's success is a dedication to the strength she insisted in me. I promise to take care of myself and carry your spirit with me. Your love stays with me every moment, and your strength guides my every step. Your blessings are upon me always. The quiet ache of missing you remains beyond words.

The reason I picked up the pen again.

Vishwas Tripathi, your unwavering belief, your constant encouragement, and the simple message, "Waiting from so long—a fan," brought life back to words. I remember my reply: "Tripathi Ji, the wait will be worth it."

This book is the promise fulfilled. Thank you for lighting the fire.

To my brother, Tushar, thank you for being my all-time support. Your steadfast dedication and care made the journey possible.

I owe immense gratitude also to my dear friend Aditi Rawat. Her steady guidance navigated me through the most crucial, and often complex, stages of the publishing process. Thank you, Aditi, for believing in this book and for providing the precise help that ensured its successful debut.

And to my incredible friends— Riya Aggarwal, Pragun, Tanya Bhati, Bidyarani, and Anjali Sahani—thank you for the laughter, the reality checks, and for always celebrating every small victory. You are the best kind of mainstays.

To Isha Jain: You hold a credit somewhere for this book however you betrayed my trust and stabbed my back. So, the next time I gave you my chest and you did not hesitate to stab again. I wish you would have been worth the gratitude I wanted to express. You once commanded the highest position in my gratitude. Yet, you labored so fiercely to erase your own worth that, having reached the minus, there is simply nothing left to appreciate.

To my cousin, Urvashi Thakur, your silliness brought me to my first book, which I never imagined. I was in a stressful mode because of you, and a realization born out of that situation made me start writing about something. My pen soon diverted to a different story, and here it is. Nevertheless, everything makes sense at the end. So, yes thank you buddy.

And finally, to my family—my truest heart's support—and to every reader: this book was written for you, and I hope it finds a permanent place on your shelf.

CONTENTS

Rain, Delay, Sky, Destiny, You 1

Willed by the Cosmos.................... 8

When Thunder Spoke, He Listened 9

The Question Beneath the Question 14

The Things That My Breath Told Him 16

Even When I Told Him About Trivedi 17

We Prayed for Our Families 19

The Jealousy of Him 22

The Denial That Wanted Me Still 24

The Musician and the Moonlight 27

Do You Remember, Shaivi? *31*

When the Noon Meets Moon *33*

The Love That Never Left *40*

Already Halfway Undone 44
Always the Love 48
Almost, Again 53
Us 59
Eyes Don't Lie 86
Departure 98

Even If I Break, Truth Must Stand *100*

At Her Doorstep 105
The Morning After 110

Rain, Delay, Sky, Destiny, You

Some stories don't knock.
They rain. They reroute.
And then... they reply to your story.

It started with rain a night before, Relentless.
The kind that soaks not just the city, But your will to move.

Everything shut—roads drowned, Deliveries vanished.
And I?
I sat hungry.
Like really hungry.
The kind of hunger that makes you question life and bread in the same breath.

ONDC gave me one option—Schedule it for tomorrow.
Okay.
Maybe food will find me when the sun does.
But noon arrived with empty hands, No food, no call — just silent plans.

Then rang a voice, my closest friend,
"Let's lunch outside, let hunger end."

That meal, a spark beyond the plate, A sign of fate, a twist of fate.
Felt like God had something more,
Because the ride that followed after Opened an old, unfinished door.

But the real twist? It came after.

To metro, Uber bike, I chose,
Though rickshaw's path was calm and close.

But something in me didn't want detours today. Not on the road, Not in life.

The rider handed me a helmet—And suddenly, I remembered Rudra.
How he used to fix it gently upon my head, Like even in a rush, he had time for silent care that words unsaid.
I plugged in music—Trying not to plug into memories. But the song did its own thing.

"Pehle bhi main tumse mila hoon..." — familiar tune —
Of meetings under silver moon:
And every line? Especially the verse:
"Ghalat kya, sahi kya, mujhe na pata hai
Tumhein 'gar pata ho, bata dena
Main arse se khud se zara laapata hoon Tumhein 'gar miloon

to pata dena" Felt like a voiceover of my past.
My heart?
Didn't ask for this rerun.

I'd started smoking—his soft plea: *"Shaivi, please, just quit for me."*
I crushed the smoke with nod so firm, his eyes held care beyond the term.
I threw it away, even as his friends teased—he just looked—like I was still his person.

Still his pulse.
I was still his truth. His gaze steady, more commanding:
"Quit it completely." I nodded then.
Today, I still smoke,
but would quit again, if he just said it. Once.

Back to the present—
So, I stopped the song, looked at the sky, it's beautiful.
White clouds soft like a sign. Clicked a picture, paused over captions, worried if words would read like a message to him.
No poems, no quotes —
Wrote *"sky is beautiful"* just fine.

But the universe was not done yet. He appeared—among top DMs.

My heart?
Skipped.
Stopped. Ran.

Notification said: *"replied to your story – yeh nee..."* And my mind raced:
Yeh neech harkat toh nahi likha? 😭

I open it.
He said:
"Yeh neeche jo frame mein ladki hai, yeh bhi beautiful hai."

🥹

A smile cracked my anxious lips. I teased back, "😂 *haraami baccha, mujhe bas (ye neech) tak dikh rha tha — Kya 'ye neech harkat' toh nahi likha tune?"* Laughter spilled between us, the ice slowly melting.

What a curveball.
Laughter floods the anxiety.
We banter.
I tease his story back—
Rain. An uncle in underwear on terrace— *"Your intentions look suspicious,"* I say. 😏

He laughs.
Replies.
Replies again. And suddenly...

We're talking. Again.

As if no silence ever happened.
As if we didn't fall apart.
As if I didn't cry the night he stopped replying.

"Uncle ko aise record kar raha hai, Irade theek nahi lag rahe," said I.
He smiled, *"Uncle ke saamne beti bhi hai, Tujhe uncle hi dikhe, oh my!"*

Then came the words, an open door, his address sent—a hopeful lore: **"Flat X, Building XXX, X view,
Come anytime, the door's for you."**
"Bin bulaye nahi," I replied,
"If welcomed, then I'll step inside."
He said, *"You're welcome, home is here, though naughty vibes may linger near."*

I smiled.
But also...
Paused.
Because when a boy who became a memory
offers you his door again, you don't walk in blindly. But you do stand there for a moment, with one hand on the doorknob, and the other... holding your heartbeat.

And just like that, the gates reopened with metaphors and grace. A half-invite, a full confession, a poem written on his face.

The hunger's gone, the rain has ceased, yet something more has been released. a message, laughter, sky so wide, a chance for hearts to once more collide.

For sometimes rain will wash away,
the past that's stuck in shades of gray.

And skies will send a whispered call — that sometimes love can conquer all.

And maybe skies and rain and songs,
are messengers dressed in disguise—may be God doesn't always knock... sometimes, he texts and says:

"Surprise."

WILLED BY THE COSMOS

I sat with echoes soft and near,
Fresh off a call I never thought I'd hear. Confused, a little — but clearer too, not random, not passing — he felt true. No flinch in words, no careless thread, he spoke like memories never fled. Not just a wind that came and went, but like the sky that always meant. I scrolled through stars on impulse slight, a horoscope in late-night light. **"What you manifest will come,"** it read — a whisper where my doubt had led.
I muttered, *"No, I will not try,"* Afraid to wish beneath this sky.
But something stirred — a quiet ache,
I realized: I'd wished while wide awake.

The way he said my name that night, the silence blooming soft and right.
Without incense, spell, or sacred flame, I'd manifested just the same.
Together — not in grand parade, but in the way that prayers are made.
In every line, each of it,
In pauses where no words would fall.
My breath had shaped a prayer so slight,

— *Shivani Singh*

When Thunder Spoke, He Listened

(A Continuation of Rain, Delay, Sky, Destiny, You)

It was raining outside— Not the soft, romantic kind, but the,
kind that bangs on glass like it's knocking at your breakdown.
Thunder cracked,
Lightening sliced through silence,
And somewhere in that storm—
I was seated in office, night shift mode,
wearing a headset,
juggling chaos,
while chaos waited back home too.
Calls spiked,
escalations poured,
and on the other side of the city, so did my family's patience.
Everything was reaching an edge. One more step, and it was
the end.
I had just tonight.
To hold it all.
To fix, to fold, to figure it out.
I paused for a while,

With every thought that we had bled.

But then it came — a colder breeze, The kind that wraps around your knees. That soft, unspoken, ghostly cost, The feeling that to gain means lost. I have to pay for every flame, To every wish that speaks your name. A price — not named, but deeply known, That love like this is never thrown. And though he feels like fate anew, I sense a storm is coming too.

It comes in storms, it comes in grace, It carves your soul, it shifts your place. Still, I feel it — what might be, A thread that ties eternally.
Our past like constellations old— Familiar paths in skies gone cold.
And though I tremble at the price, My heart still walks that edge of ice.

For some love stories, though delayed, Return like sunsets never fade. I didn't plan to ask for this, But love arrives like gentle mist. And now I stand, a wish come true, In quiet debt... to skies and you.
The universe, it heard my trust —
And maybe... maybe it's manifesting us. Now, I silenced the thoughts and called him first as he said
And he picked up...
On the first ring.
As if he was already waiting.
Funny, how we observe the smallest things
in people we love— The pace of their breath,
The softness in their voice,

The pause between "hello" and "are you okay?"
I noticed it all.
Noted it like scripture.
And then, I spoke.
Spilled.
About debts and deadlocks,
About love that was fraying, Family breaking, My breath aching.
He listened.
Not just to the words— But the weight behind them.
The sighs between syllables.
The silence I didn't say aloud.
And when I finished,
Tears pooled quietly inside my tone,
He simply said—
"You'll do it. I know." And I believed him.
Not because I believed in myself, But because he believed in me. And that... was enough.
Stupid maybe,
But that's love.
We start believing not in fate,
but in the voice that says,
"Even now, even this... you can carry." Thunder faded.
Storms outside began to sleep.
But a new calm brewed within me—
The kind born not from solutions, But from someone who stayed and simply listened when the thunder spoke.

And then he asked—
"Okay... but apart from all that, how are *you*?" Just like that.

As if the wreckage could be separated from the soul.
I hesitated. Said, "I'm fine." He paused.
"Are you sure?"
I nodded in my breath.
He didn't buy it.
"Don't lie."
What could I even say?
How do you explain to someone— that the only moment you truly feel *fine* is *when they're around*?
That joy, relief, love—even the will to keep going— have all started wearing *his name* as a middle name? That when everything else feels hollow, his presence fits perfectly into the shape of that emptiness?
How do you tell someone:
You are the part of my life that feels alive.
When you're here, the noise dims. The ache pauses.
And even if nothing changes outside— everything inside starts to breathe again.
But I didn't say any of that.
I just let the silence hold it.
He didn't press.
Maybe he knew.
Maybe love doesn't always need explaining.
Sometimes, presence is proof enough.
And still... he has them all now— the friends,
the girl I once called my sister, the circle I once belonged to.
All connected through me.
She knew.
She knew I could never unlove him.
But she still chose him.

They all did.
Lied.
Left.
He might have it all now— but not love. Not *this* love. Not the kind that drips like honey into grief, that aches like poetry written in your blood.
The kind of love

that doesn't just wait— it survives.
He can find any woman. But to feel what *I* make him feel, he'll need a woman who is me.
And there's no second version of this storm and softness.
Tonight, on that call, he forgot the walls he built.
He crossed them.
He let me in.
And though he never said "I love you," his silence wore it on its sleeve. Because we were and we are— unfinished sentences meant to be reread.
And maybe the world rewrote us, but it never un-wrote our truth.

THE QUESTION BENEATH THE QUESTION

Then came his pause, followed by a question dressed in nonchalance—

"Have you started liking someone lately?"
I smiled the way silence does
before thunder. **"No,"** I said—
firm, like a door refusing to open
to a world that isn't him. He
asked again. This time softer,
but with that tilt in his voice—
curious, but not for the answer.
**"Someone in office, maybe?
Someone your eyes now wait
to meet?"** It wasn't about know-
ing.

It was about *hoping*.
Not that I had, but
that I hadn't. He
didn't ask twice for in-
formation. He asked
because he needed to
still be mine.

Even if he never said it out loud.
And that's the thing— you start
recognizing the tremble beneath
people's questions when you love
them enough to read the spaces
between their words.

He was hoping

I hadn't healed. That no one else
was warming the room where
he once breathed. He claimed
I was always the one too deep,
too involved, too much. But that
night, his voice betrayed him.
Because sometimes jealousy isn't
loud. Sometimes it's just a quiet
prayer that you still belong.

And God, if only he
knew— How I have
walked past thousand eyes
and still looked for just
his.

How my heart still
stops breathing at
the thought of him
smiling at someone
else the way he used
to with me. He
can pretend this is
casual.

But I've loved him enough
to know: That night,
he wasn't wondering if
I'd moved on. He was
afraid I had.

THE THINGS THAT MY BREATH TOLD HIM

I said **no**— but it wasn't just the word. It was the way my voice didn't flinch, the way the silence after it felt like home.

My eyes in that moment—
had he seen them, he'd never
question again. But even
without sight, he saw. Be-
cause love, when real, travels.

It breathes between the lines,
tiptoes in the quiet, and lingers
in the air like perfume he once
gifted me and forgot.

We were just on a call.

No eyes, no glances. Just
my breath and his ears. But
he heard it— the unspoken
poetry of how his name still
lives in my exhale. He knew.

He just *knew.*

That I hadn't gone anywhere. That
no one else stood where he once
did. He asked, but my breath al-
ready answered. And maybe that's
the thing about love like ours—
You don't always need to be seen
to be understood. Sometimes, you

just need to breathe the same space
for a second longer than necessary.

And that's how he knew:
Even now, he was still the
only one my heart paused
for.

EVEN WHEN I TOLD HIM ABOUT TRIVEDI

Rudra asked again— for the twentieth time, like repetition might bend the truth my love refused to break. "Is there someone new?" As if the answer might change the more he heard it. As if repetition could bend the truth my love refused to break.

I sighed.

"Out of 900 people," I said,
"these eyes still know one face."
And then, casually,

I told him about
Saurav Trivedi—

I told him about Saurav *Trivedi*—
the guy who shows up in scenes I
never write him into.

Same surname. Similar
fate.

Different story. Funny, isn't it? The universe likes to play doppelgänger with names when it can't recreate hearts. "He's engaged," I said, "Still somehow walks into my life

without reason." And I laughed.

Because I had no room in me to welcome coincidences that weren't you. Even my friends grew worried— what if he falls for me? And there, through the call, a silence. Not of disinterest, but of jealousy, bubbling beneath the voice that once told me he didn't care.

You see, jealousy has a funny way of confessing what ego won't say. And Rudra—

he was quiet for a second too long.

I smiled.

Because the man who claimed it was just me loving him, was suddenly protective of a space he never quite left. I didn't need to spell it out. He knew I was full— of *him*, still. And no Trivedi,

no coincidence, no crowd of
900 could make room in eyes
already overflowing.

WE PRAYED FOR OUR FAMILIES

And then, I changed
the thread from hearts
to home. "How's your
mom?"

I asked, softly. The kind of
soft that tiptoes between wor-
ry and warmth.

"She's good," he said,
"But not fine." Words that stood
on the edge of truth— brave, yet
breaking. I knew what he meant.
She's still holding on, but not in
the way she used to. He said it
lightly, but I heard the heaviness
in the way his breath curved
around hope. She's better, but
not recovering.

There are barely chances, he said.
And in that pause, I felt him.

Not the voice in my ear— but
the boy in him, longing for
a hug he'll never ask for. I

could hear the sighs he tried to suppress, the grief that sat too quietly in his throat. So I held him in words. "Tujhe ghar jaana chahiye," I said, gently insistent.

More than once.

More than lightly.

Because sometimes love is not just saying *I miss you,* it's reminding someone to return to their roots before it's too late. I emphasized more. Because sometimes, what they need is not advice— but someone to *care enough* to repeat it.

And in that moment, between thunder outside and storm inside him— we sat together, in a silence full of unsaid prayers. He asked,

"How's your grandmother?" He remembered.

Even after silence had crept between us for months that turned into seasons— he remembered. The same way I remembered his mother's unspoken pain. We were two people still holding space for people we've

never met, but always cared for because we
cared for each other. And so we prayed—

for the old hearts that shaped us.
For the strength of bloodlines
that sometimes feel too fragile
to carry our weight. There was
something sacred in that pause.

Two former lovers murmur-
ing hope into the same uni-
verse, for families that were
quietly breaking. And then,
I told him something that
once fractured me. About
the boy before him. The first
heart

that taught me what it means
to hurt and to hope in the same
breath. The one who never real-
ly knew how much his presence
shifted my inner tides. How deeply
I longed for him to just stay. It had
been over a year and a half since
I'd moved on— but this was the
first time we'd met since everything
happened. Almost three years. And
somehow, when I stood before him
again, there was no sting.

No longing.

Just closure.

And I shared that with Rudra. Not for validation— but for truth. For honesty, because in that moment, he deserved nothing less than the whole version of me.

THE JEALOUSY OF HIM

I told him— about
the boy I met.

The one who once made my heart ache before I even knew what ache meant. About the coffee, the conversation, how years had passed but civility returned like muscle memory. I told him—not to hurt him, but to help him understand that I am trying.

That I am meeting people.

That I do not wear my grief like armor anymore. I wanted him to be relieved— that I'm not stuck.

That I don't wait by the window every
time it rains.

But I also knew... That somewhere in him, a muscle tightened. Not because I had moved on— but because I hadn't, and still, someone else got a seat across from me.

I saw it in his pauses. The little silence that tiptoed between questions.

He claimed to the world:

"I don't love her
But love isn't always what we say.
Sometimes it's in how many times you ask

if my eyes are still searching. Sometimes it's in the jealousy you pretend you don't feel.

But I see it.

I always do.

And still,

I gave him that story— not as proof that I'm better, not to make him chase— But because the truth between people like us deserves to stay undressed. He doesn't get to claim me, but he flinches when someone else looks too long.

And me?

I carry the quiet pride of knowing that no matter who sits across from me— It's still your name that lives inside my breath.

THE DENIAL THAT WANTED ME STILL

A boy I long since let go.

When that meeting happened, sure— but nothing remained.

Nothing but a reminder that
no one ever felt like *him.* he
couldn't hide it. The quiet sigh.

The faltering tone. The invisible
weight in his breath when I told him
I'm meeting people now. He has
it all— friends I introduced him
to, the girl who knew I loved
him and chose him anyway.

They betrayed.

They left. They stayed—
with *him.* And still— he
holds this hollow. This
space I once filled so deep-
ly that even now it echoes
in his laughter.

He doesn't say he loves me.
But he wants me untouched.

Unclaimed. As if love can be
owned by those who won't
confess it.

And I?

I can't unlove him. He is the sky I
breathe, the sea my soul was poured
into. No matter how many paths
he takes To walk away from me—
somehow, he always returns. And
tonight—

beneath thunder and shattered timing—
he asked, then asked again, as if he needed
to hear what my heart has always known:
That no other name can ever taste the
way his does on the tip of my prayer. He
speaks like a stranger pretending he never
touched the stars we named together. He
says—

"It must've happened." You and
that boy. The night, the hormones,
the body's gravity pulling close.

He speaks of science.

Of chances.

Of how physicality finds its way between warmth and wine.

But his voice?

It trembled.

And I know him.

I know the slight crack
his words try to seal. The
catch in his breath when his
imagination dares to place
someone else where he shall
belong.

He wants to sound neutral.

Detached.

Like an old friend hearing old news.

But he fails.

God, he fails. Because love
like ours doesn't vanish with
silence.

It hides.

But it pulses like a second heartbeat.
He says I loved him alone— that this
bond was mine to feel. But why then
does his voice tighten when my story
includes another name? Why then,

do his questions multiply like doubts
blooming on ground he swore was
barren?

And I knew— I
always knew—

This wasn't just *my* love. It
was *our* echo. Souls don't
lie, and ours?

They keep finding each other at the
bend of every ending. He ran, but
the universe pulled him back.

He tried logic.

But love breaks rules.

And even in denial, his silence
whispered— I'm still the story
he wants no one else to tell.

THE MUSICIAN AND THE MOONLIGHT

(But My Heart Stayed Elsewhere)

I told him everything— the meeting
I could've kept quiet, but didn't.

Because I knew— it would stir
something in him. That familiar
ache, the one he hides behind

nonchalance and logic. I lied at
work, took a half-day.

Rapido through rain and nerves.
He stood there waiting— that boy
from the past, now a man with
a guitar, and unspoken hopes.
Inside,

instruments lined the corners—
music in the air, his friends
smiling soft, the vibe unfiltered.
He brought water—

two glasses, one cold, one warm.
"I didn't know what you prefer."
That made me laugh. How could
something so small feel so tender?
We jammed—

notes, laughter, wind.
Then the terrace— smoke
curling in breeze, walls
under us, sky above.

He said,

"You don't open up easily." I
paused.

Because once— with
him—

I was an open book

spilling poems,
secrets, silly jokes.
Rudra and I, we
didn't jam.

We *collided.*
Roasting and rhythm.

Staring and silence.

Ink and intimacy. Now I write
verses on him, while he pens
lines in diaries he won't let me
read. Later— he handed me a
guitar, fingers tracing chords,

softly guiding mine.

Then a film, *Rockstar*.

Then talk. He told me about France, a contract he'd been waiting for.
And then—*ding*— the
mail arrived.

His eyes lit up.

He said I'm lucky.
I smiled but said nothing.
Because I didn't want him to
hold on to me like I'm hope
when I can't return it.

Not now.

Not honestly.

Twilight leaked in through curtains.

He said he used to dance—salsa.
And so we danced, feet uncer-
tain, hands unsure, his heart near,
mine... elsewhere.

We laid side by side.

No threads tied.

No sparks.

Just breath.

He asked for a hug. I
said no. But then—

I gave in.

Just a moment.

But even that...
felt like a betrayal to a love that
wouldn't leave me.

Later, I told Rudra everything.

Each detail.

Each hesitation.

He asked if something happened.

His voice too steady, but not quite.
His silence too sharp to be neutral.

Why would he ask if
he didn't care? Why
would he burn if he
had no flame?

But even in the arms of another,
all I could think of was *him*.

The one who never claimed me,
yet somehow never let me go.

DO YOU REMEMBER, SHAIVI?

He spoke of hormones, science
wrapped in logic, like love could
be decoded into chemicals and
chance.

But I stopped him—

*Hormones alone don't bring me close. My
body doesn't move where my heart doesn't
follow."*

He fell silent. And
then,

with a shift in breath and a quieter voice, he
asked—

"Do You Remember, Shaivi?"

No name. No
place.

No scene.

But I knew.

God, I knew.

That one moment, hanging like
unfinished poetry between us for
months—
Our eyes locked, our breath in sync, the
silence louder than any confession.

He was so sure I'd know.
And he was right.

Because when it's *him*,
I don't need context—
I just *feel*.

His voice didn't ask for a memory.
It asked for a truth.

Would it have been different,
if it was me instead of him?
Would you have said yes, let go,
let me in... finally?

He didn't say it, but I heard it
in every pause.

And my silence in return— was
not denial, but a thousand un-
said yeses wrapped in the ache of
restraint.

Because love never left.

Desire never died.

Only distance grew.

But even now— with new names,
new spaces— we're still standing
on that edge.

Remembering the almost, and
wondering

if it still waits for us to finish
what we never began.

WHEN THE NOON MEETS MOON

(The Black Kurta memory he was talking about)

It was one of those days
when my heart chose No logic, no text sent ahead— just a tug from within that said, *go right away.* I walked to my first

Eterna Hello

office, no reason, no cue, just a lunch-hour impulse under a restless sky's hue. My friends weren't expecting, none had a clue—

I stood outside, pacing fast, anxious
heartbeat breaking through.

plugged into a song on loop—

"Yoon Shabnami pehle nahi thi chandani, dekho chaand aaya, chaand nazar aaya..." The song echoed through my breath, each line syncing with my pulse, That rhythm echoed something more— a yearning, a sign, a pull.

"Dekho chaand aaya, chaand nazar aaya... Aaya, aaya, aaya..."

And just like the moon obeying the lyrics, he
came out of the exit gate— **Rudra.**

And oh... *he* was wearing a **black kurta**.

Black.

At office.

With no occasion. Dashing, radiant— he looked like the embodiment of the moonlight I was just listening to.

Like the song had summoned him.

He didn't expect to see me.
I didn't expect to see him like *that*.
It was a feast for my eyes.

Our eyes sparkled—glistening with something unnamed.

Both of us... *blushing.*
Like the universe had lit a soft halo over that very moment.

I asked, "What made you wear this today?" He said, **"I just listened to my heart."** He asked what brought me here to office today.

I said - likewise. I also listened to my heart.

As we walked towards the food stall, **Madhav**—my friend—teased me.

"Khul gayi na."
He said it in a slang tone, playful, mischievous.

I pretended not to understand.

So he repeated it again.
I said, "No." And he smirked:

"Teri aankhon mein dikh raha hai."
And damn it— he wasn't wrong. My eyes *were* full of Rudra They always had been.

Shining like they'd seen their moon in daylight.

Then time moved again.

He had to go. Back to the inside, to
the world that didn't have me in it. We
shook hands—

but it wasn't just a handshake.
Not the kind colleagues share in passing.

Not the kind friends offer casually.

It was... more. A holding, a knowing,
a confession without sound. He
didn't just grasp my hand; he held it—
firm, warm, lingering— like he didn't
want to let go.

Like something unsaid had finally found a voice through the quiet press of palms.

His thumb brushed ever so slightly across the back of my hand, a delicate gesture, but loaded—flirting at the edge of confession.

He didn't let go.
Neither did I.

Eyes, chico... they don't lie.
And his?

Were poems—

undone and unfolding.

There was no one else in that moment—

just us,

breathing in the weight of what we are, of
what we might've been

if only timing, pride, or fear hadn't stood in the way.
A friend broke the trance—

"Bhai Rudra, aaj haath nahi chhorhna kya Shaivi ka?" Everyone laughed.

He smiled sheepishly, reluctantly loosening his grip, but
I could feel it— he didn't want to.

Neither did I.

He finally let go.

Walked back into the office.

And I?

I walked away too— legs
moving,

heart still behind, thinking—

Why does he hide it so well,
when his hands confess what
his lips never tell?
Why does he keep pretending?
Why avoid what's written in your eyes, hands, your heartbeat?
Why act like we're nothing when *everything* about
us feels like *everything*?

There's an invisible string between us.

We've tried to deny it.
Ignore it.

Break it.

But it stretches back—every single time.

A pull, like the tide to the moon.

Like fate.

I don't know.
wondering—

why must love wear masks of silence?

Why must someone who holds this much in his heart act like there's nothing at all?

There's an invisible string between us— And to be honest—

if that day, he hadn't walked
back inside, if we had just...
taken a walk,

talked in some quiet space, gone somewhere with no walls, no people, no pretending...

Maybe we'd still be there— hand in hand, soul beside soul, not just remembering what we were— but becoming what we could've been. And It wouldn't have been a bad idea.

THE LOVE THAT NEVER LEFT

Do you remember, Shaivi?" he said,
Though the yes was in my head. I
paused, let him pull the thread— Let
his words be softly led.

"Madhav ne bola tha, khul gayi na?"
Main black kurta pehan ke aaya tha...".
That day lives rent-free in my soul,
The way he looked... completely whole.

I love him, so of course I knew,

But he chose another—what else is new? Still
he remembered, word for word, Every glance,
every whisper heard. So back to now—when
he brought this up, With pauses, soft and
slow. Why would he recall so much, If he had
truly let me go?

So I asked him, "Why bring this now?" He
smirked, a glimmer on his brow.

"If I wear that kurta for you again,
Will your heart still melt like then?"
He meant—if he had been the one,

Instead of the boy I'd only just begun
To know, in another time, another scene, Would
our love have turned serene?

I dodged the curve, I changed the beat, "How
do you know Madhav's discreet? He whis-

pered that in my ear that day..." "He told me later," he tried to say.

I said, "Oh please, you over-heard.
You watch me close—you catch each word."
He laughed and paused, his voice went low,

"It's been 1.5 years, but still I know." Each pause contained unsaid things, Like letters lost with broken wings.

Still he asked, with teasing grace,

"Tell me now—would you melt in place?"
"What good will my answer do?"
I smiled, yet my heart still knew—.
He picked someone else, yet seeks my fire,

Still checks to see if I still admire. I left my first job just to heal, To blur his face, to mute the feel. But then again, in the next job too, He returned—and all that grew.
He left for weeks, and the air grew dry,
The office turned into a hollow sky. Even in silence, he filled the space, Like a ghost I'd never dare replace.

Now he asks, "Will you still sway?"
I said, "Wear the black kurta, we'll see that day."
Then he went soft, heart beating slow,

"Like I miss my ex... do you miss me though?"
I asked him, "Why are you asking now?"

He said, "Just like that..." (but I know somehow.)
He needed proof I still reside

In the space where his truths used to hide.

So I gave him all I had in me—
"Rudra, yaad unko kiya jata hai
Jinko bhool gaye ho kabhi. But
you?

You're in my every breath,

Like the sky around me, till death." He went
quiet, but stayed near, Asked again what he
longed to hear. "Why did you leave Warby
Parker then?" This time, I told him. No pre-
tend. The call kept stretching, hearts afloat,
Woven into every note.

He said again, "Come over soon." The
clock was ticking past the moon.

It was time to log out, I packed my bag,

The sky outside? A stormy drag.

"It's raining like mad," I softly said, But
he didn't want the call to be dead. "I'll
stay on, even if you're mute," He said
with charm, oddly cute.

"When are you coming?"—asked once more,
"Saturday?"—he opened the door. "I'll let you

know," I calmly sighed, And in that moment, I nearly cried.

For not even a month had passed me by Since I prayed beneath that mountain sky. In Kainchi Dham, with folded hands, Where magic moves and love expands.

It felt surreal,

Since I'd prayed beneath that hill— And here he was, back in my life, Without a forceful will.

we speak again, we breathe— A miracle spun from wounds beneath. I closed my eyes and thanked the stars, Paused my heart, hid all the scars. Because tomorrow's storm had work for me, But tonight, love flowed unexpectedly. And maybe some bonds defy the fate, You think you're done—then they await.

— *Shivani Singh*

Already Halfway Undone

Hi Rudra, I typed,
Shall I come today?
A pause. A pulse.
What will you cook for me?
Simple words, but wrapped
in the hope of being near him
again.

He answered with gentle insistence—
"Please come.
Tell me, what do you want?"
I said, *"Anything."* Because with
him,
because in his presence, hunger fades— only
craving remains.

I left it open,
"Anything."

He insisted—
"Shall I get something packed?"
Time slipped quietly by, The screen lit up again— **"Are you coming?"**
I told him,

"Yes, About to board metro." "How long till you arrive?" "An hour," I whispered.
An hour to close the distance between two beating hearts.

"What will you like to have?" he asked again, as if the food wasn't the hunger in question.

"Anything you'll have," I replied. *"You'll surely eat?"* he teased. *"Yes,"* I said softly, *"Whatever you choose."* Our playful banter— a language only we understood.

He answered—
"Taunts."
I replied—
"Works."

"And apart from food?" "Anything," I said.

"Think twice." he warned.
I was certain—*"Done."*
He pressed, **"What?"**
And I—knowing exactly what he meant—
replied with a mirrored tease, *"What, what?"*

But beneath the playful echo, my breath
hitched.

Because I knew— he wasn't
asking about food, or time, or
place.

He was asking if I'd still let the night
curl its fingers around my spine, if I'd
come close enough to feel the heat of
his skin without pulling away. He was
asking if I'd let him near, in the way
only lovers once do— wordless, slow,
where memory becomes touch again.
my breath already answering *yes*.

And I said *"What, what"* because
I couldn't say,
I'm already on my way—
not just through the city, but back
to you.

"Come fast," he typed,
"I need to leave for Madhav's."

"Who goes at midnight?" I asked.

"Friend invited. So I must."
He asked,
"How will you come after the metro?" "You come," I said. He replied— *"Acha ji."*

"If not, Uber bike's there."
He warned—
"Not safe at night."
"That's why I said, you come."

He sent another
"?"
"What's in it for me?" he wrote.

I countered and I smiled into the phone:
"What do you want?" He
said— *"Come first.*
We'll then see." And as I read
him between the pauses, my face
lit up— a glow I hadn't worn
in seasons, and my eyes... they
found their spark again. And I left
home— already halfway undone.

— *Shivani Singh*

Always the Love

It was the evening that sighed like a secret, The city tired, and I—**freed from the storm.** Hair brushed back by a rebellious wind, *vulnerability—quietly worn.*

No message yet, but I still got ready.
Cleaned myself gently, with the kind of
care *Maybe he'd want me. Maybe*

I'd let him.

A lie I lived to guard my truth,
Took leave from duty, chose love instead. No
word from him, yet I prepared— **Hope, like
jasmine, bloomed in my head.**

The metro hummed with nervous breath,
The wind played with my hair, like it was

trying to tell me— *something is about to begin,* or maybe, *just return.*

The wind touched my face
the way he would. I clicked a
selfie—

not because I looked good, but because I
felt something rare.

Diet Mountain Dew on trembling lips.

And then he came.
On that same old bike—Dhanno—his loyal steed
with the same boyish charm that once made a girl
believe **the world could be gentle.**

My heart lurched with each road's dip.
He asked me to hold him.
He didn't know I never really let go.
The road was bumpy.
So was everything between us.

His friend called.
He lied.
Said he was elsewhere. And
somehow,
that lie made it feel more sacred.
In that little lie,
I felt the truth—
this was ours.

He showed me his go-to coffee house. I'd
seen it before— on stories that weren't mine.
But tonight, he was.

His mole near the neck, a silent lure, My
fingers ached to trace the skin, to slip
closer, rest my restless head against his
shoulder,

I clicked a photo—his shirt, not face, For memories
fear the sound of names. A water bottle spoke of
betrayal's weight, And yet, he smiled like nothing
changed.

At his place— to a friendship I
lost. "Remember this bottle?"

I did.
I just said "hmm" and swallowed
everything else.

Dinner tasted like unfinished songs, Clock
was ticking, but silence was loud. My soul sat
beside me, holding back— Not to cry. Not to
plead. Not to be proud.

We went to the terrace.
The sky didn't ask questions.
Neither did we. The stars
looked down,
kind—quiet—

like they knew not to interrupt two
hearts relearning how to beat beside
each other.

After so long, we stood close enough to feel each
other breathe, yet far enough to keep the truth from
trembling out.

He kept looking at me. Not just
looking— studying, as if my
breath carried verses he'd been
dying to read.

My gaze traced the map of him— the
curve of his silence, the rhythm of his
restraint.

And I—
I kept turning away, but not
really.

My soul was already leaning in, answering
him in every skipped heartbeat, every shaky
inhale that tasted like longing.

I saw him— not with my eyes, but through my
pulse, through the tremble that lived between still-
ness and surrender.

My soul spilled— *unfiltered, undone,*
entirely his.

So I looked away, not out of
strength— but because I knew
he'd see the part of me that never
stopped choosing him.

And he'd see it— the love I still cradle like a
fragile flame, the ache I've turned into poet-
ry, and the girl who holds her whole world
in the quiet surrender of his stare.

His eyes whispered it softly, like a secret meant
only for my heart to hear, pausing between words
as if they carried a thousand unsaid prayers.

I didn't ask if he did— some questions are
too sacred to touch, and sometimes, some
answers and the purest kind of love *lives
quietly.*

It just lingers— like moonlight on skin, like
breath that almost becomes a kiss— in the
hush between two hesitant hearts that still
remember how to care.

And in that silence between us, where words once
faltered, I found a quiet truth— that sometimes love
is not loud, but lives in the space where we still dare
to hope.

— *Shivani Singh*

Almost, Again

And two people—Rudra and Shaivi—
who had business to pretend to not look at
each other like *that*... after everything.

After time, distance, silence.
But there we were again, on the
terrace.

Midnight wrapped around us like old comfort.
The wind teased, but not as much as we did.
The star's gaze was wild, but not wilder than the
energy between us.

He kept looking at me.
Not casually.
Like he was reading the rhythm of my skin.
And I kept looking away.
But not really.

Every cell in me was already responding to him. She saw him through her breath, through my silence, through the way my heart skipped a beat around him.

Layers in laughter.
Flirt hidden in wit.
Desire masked in punchlines.
And then he dropped it, softly, playfully, purposefully: *"If I wear that black kurta again... will you... melt again?"*

We both knew what he meant.
Not just physically.
But emotionally.
Would I melt again?
Would I give in again? He meant my walls, my skin, my want.

That I'd always melt a little in his presence.

I smirked. Played it safe.
"Wear it first, will see then."
He replied, with that glint in his eyes— *"Sure. Anyway, it has to come off."*

Oh, he knew.
He knew how easily I could unravel for him.

And that night, I wasn't pretending otherwise.

Let him wear it first. Let my
eyes feast

before the fire begins.

Because that kurta on him?
It's a sin I'd willingly worship.

And there it was— that truth
neither of us dared to admit in full
sentences.

That yes, I wanted him.
That yes, he wanted me too.
That what they shared was mutual.
Electric.
And still very much alive.

But desire wasn't loud.
It whispered.
In glances.
In pauses.
In the way we still hadn't said goodbye, not really.

I replied,
"No worries, you wear first." What I
didn't say: Seeing him in that black
kurta would light up my eyes.

And if it ended up on the floor after—so be it. Let desire take its course.

He said it's in his cupboard.
We turned toward the room.

And the stairs— those stairs were
new to my feet.

But his presence?

So achingly familiar.

Now, silence walked beside us.

That night, we walked differently. A gap
between our hands, but not between
our intentions.

I wanted his hand. I want-
ed that warmth again, the
safety, the spark.

But I stayed still.
Afraid to ask.
Afraid it wouldn't be the same.

And then— like a twist written by the universe— fate twisted my ankle.

Pain shot through. And before I
could fall, he caught me.

His hand found mine, not
as an act— as instinct.

The kind of instinct that only comes from
love once lived.

And in that moment— we paused.

Time slipped.
So did my breath. His grip was strong, but
not just on my hand—on my heart.

My soul remembered. Our eyes
locked. And for a breathless mo-
ment, I wasn't standing on stairs.
I was floating inside a feeling I'd
been starving for— his warmth.

And we stood there, in a dark staircase, with
nothing but everything between us.

Then we walked. But
this time, he didn't let
go.

And I didn't want him to.

The stairs didn't just carry us downward.
We undressed our denial.
We saw what we weren't saying.

That we were still two bodies made
of memory and magnetism—
because in that grip, was the touch of love which
never passed, and present possibility.
And maybe even something more.

Maybe it was a new staircase.
Maybe it wasn't where we began.

But that night, those steps learned who
we were.

We all have memories in stairs. But
that night, I reminded mine... what
it felt like to be wanted, to be held,
to feel whole.

Even if just for a moment.
Even if it never happens again.

— *Shivani Singh*

Us

Now we were inside.

No more wind.

No more stairs.

Just a room *holding its breath.*

I sat on the edge of the bed,my heart pacing in *stillness*. He sat by the cupboard, pretending to look for the black kurta.

But that search was a delay. We both knew.

And then — he stopped.

Not the kind of pause meant to stall, but the kind that arrives when *something sacred demands your attention.* He looked at me. Not just with his eyes — with *everything*.

Like I was *gravity*, pulling truth from his ribs.

I looked away, again.

Not out of disinterest — but because looking at him meant *crumbling* in real time.

The silence was alive now.

It pressed into our lungs, *slow and soft like a memory slipping back into the room.*

Breath.
That was all we could hear.

He stepped closer.

And closer.

Until the space between us was just enough for *tension to stretch across.*

My eyes found his, finally.

That eye contact — it wasn't an accident. It was *everything we never said.*

And then,

in a voice that *curled into my skin*, he whispered— **"Kurte ki zarurat lag nahi rahi vaise."**

Not a question.

A statement.

A confession dressed in mischief.

I didn't smile.
Not fully.

But *my breath did.*
My body did.
Every inch of me softened in that sentence.

Because what he meant was— *You're already melting.*

I haven't even touched you yet. *You're already mine.*

Still.

The room knew.

The air thickened. Not with heat, but with history.

And in that *unspoken agreement*— where *want met want,* and the *past sat quiet in a corner, watching us almost collide again*— everything felt possible.

Even if just for *that night.* Even if just for *that look.*

And then— *no more distance.*

He closed the space between us not with words, but with touch.

His hands, familiar.

Certain.

Not asking—knowing.

Not rushing—returning.

He lifted my top, slowly, like *unveiling a memory etched beneath fabric.* His lips met my skin—

soft at first, then certain, like he'd *never truly forgotten the taste* of where my heart-beat lives.

Both hands claimed me, not in hunger, but in *recognition*.

As if saying:

"This is still mine. You are still mine."
And I—

I didn't resist.
I surrendered not just my body,
but *all the pretending.* Because in
that moment, I wasn't confused.
I wasn't afraid.

I was just a girl, *loved so deeply,*

being remembered by the same pair of hands that
once held me whole.

His face pressed into my chest
like he was *seeking home.* Not in
lust— *in longing.*

In that *desperate, aching way*
you hold on to something you
think you've lost.

And I held him back— not because I
had to, but because *my body still knew*
him— every inch.

Every rhythm. Every
reason.

In that quiet room, with no light but
the one between us, we let *memory*
become touch.

And for a moment, we were not just friends,
neither ex-lovers, nor strangers. We were just two
souls *finding each other again*— through skin,
through silence, through the parts that *never*
stopped wanting.

In one swift motion, his fingers found
the clasp— unhooked, like *muscle mem-*
ory had been waiting for this moment all
along.

And I paused.

Just for a flicker of thought.

Has he done this before?
Or was he just this sure with me?

But the thought faded beneath the *warmth of his mouth* pressing into me again.

Neck, chest,

waist— he kissed me like each place *held a story* he was *desperate to re-read.*

I breathed in gasps—
not from surprise, but
from *recognition*.

My hands moved too—

not in hesitation, but
invitation.

He unbuttoned.

I unzipped. Our
motions synced like
we had done this *in*
dreams before.

Jeans slipped away. Then the
last piece of cloth, his hand
tugging gently— one hand
claiming me, the other *wor-
shipping it.*

I melted. Not just
in body, but in
trust.

I undressed him, not like I was unveiling
lust, but like I was *freeing* something
sacred.

And now—

we stood bare.

Two bodies.

No fabric.

No lies.

No pretending.

Just breath. And
touch. And
memory

finding its voice through fin-
gertips and skin.

He looked at me like I was the
only language his body could
speak. And I looked at him
like he was *the only place* I ever
wanted to be lost in.

Because being naked isn't just
about being unclothed.

It's about *being unguarded. Unguided.*

And in that moment, we
were both exactly that. Not
just *exposed*— but *chosen.*

Again.

As bodies tangled in warmth, my
mind held one thread— loose,
quiet, but *unignorable.*

They must've broken up.

That's what I told myself as his lips traced lines of fire along
my waist,

as our breaths tangled, as my skin opened to
a love I never really shut away.

Because how could he be here like this if he still
belonged to someone else?

And yet— the
someone else used
to be mine too. A
closest friend who
knew who knew

that this boy wasn't a chapter but the whole book I never stopped reading.

Still,
no words were spoken. No questions
asked.

Not because I didn't want answers. But because in that moment, answers felt too sharp for something so soft.

I chose trust. Not
blindly— but bravely.

I chose the present. Not as
escape— but as reclamation.

Let the past stay folded for now, I thought, as his hands moved like poetry across my skin. Let this moment be its own truth, untouched by old betrayals.

But still, in the back of my mind— beneath the pleasure, beneath the calm, beneath even the rising warmth of want— a whisper remained:

What if he hasn't let her go?
What if I'm not the only one he's touching like this?
What if I'm not the only one he looks at like home?

And yet I didn't stop.

Because sometimes, love isn't about certainty. It's about choosing to be vulnerable even when every scar warns you otherwise.

So I stayed.
Unclothed.
Unasked.
Unwavering.

And the question— the one that burned quietly in my chest— would
wait.

Because tonight, I chose not to lose myself to suspicion. I chose to be felt, not feared.

I leaned in— not just with my lips, but with every silent yes my heart had tucked away for him.

Our mouths met.
Breaths aligned. A slow, sacred rhythm, like a
secret only our bodies could speak.

And in that kiss, was more
than longing.

There was memory.

There was forgiveness. There was a return to something I never truly left.

His hands travelled downward, unhurried, as if learning the language of me all over again. Fingers reached the center of me— the place no one else had ever touched.

And I let him in.

Not just physically.

But emotionally.

Spiritually. In the way only a first time can feel like a sacred offering.

He moved with care, but not caution. Like he already knew what made me unfold.

I felt it— a warmth rising in my core, an ache meeting answer, a tide pulling me further into him. And even as my body responded, so did something deeper.

Something that whispered:

"This is the first time I've let someone in this close— to my skin, my breath, my story."

Because for me, it wasn't just about desire. It was about trust. About choosing to let someone see me whole.

And in that moment, beneath his mouth, his hands, his breath— I wasn't afraid.

I was open.

And I was home.

His fingers moved through my hair—not to possess, but to soothe.

As if brushing back time itself.

And then came the question.

Low.

Steady.

Laced with care.

"Shall we move ahead, Shaivi?"

He said my name like it was a prayer.

And in that moment, we weren't just two bodies. We were two souls on the edge of something irreversible.

I looked into his eyes. Saw not just
the want— but the wait. Not just
the hunger— but the softness that
came with it.

And then, with no tremble in my voice, only
truth, I answered: **"Yes."**

And that yes—wasn't just permission.
It was a surrender.

A choice.

A beginning.

Time slowed.

Breath held itself.

The world outside that room disappeared.

Because in that eye contact, I found everything I'd ever left unsaid.

No more pretending.

No more looking away.

Just two people, finally meeting each other without masks.

And as we moved closer—skin to skin, heart to heart—the night deepened its silence, to make space for a love that had been waiting far too long.

He moved closer, his breath warm against mine, his body ready to bridge the space we'd long danced around.

And just as he tried to enter, my voice rose—not in fear, but in care.

"But we don't have protection."

A pause. A flicker of conscience against the heat of the moment.

He looked at me, his eyes not breaking from mine. And softly, he said, **"We'll manage."**

There was no pressure in his voice.

No urgency.

Just a quiet confidence that things would be okay.

I took a breath—deep, searching, half of it instinct, half of it trust.

And then I chose.

Chose to stay in that moment.

Chose to flow with it.

Not out of recklessness, but from a place where love sometimes asks you to surrender control to connection.

Because not everything is planned.

Some moments arrive like waves too strong to resist.

And we were one body now—not perfectly prepared, but perfectly willing.

The room grew quieter, except
for our rhythm.

A rhythm made of old ache, new trust, and the kind of intimacy that lives beyond the rules of logic.

We held on to each other. Not
just physically—

but like people who knew that sometimes, closeness means letting go of every script except the one your heart is writing right now.

It was a moment my body had never known—a threshold crossed with both anticipation and ache.

Pleasure arrived like a spark, but
pain was right beside it, uninvited
but honest.

I felt myself stretch—
not just in skin, but in
spirit.

And it hurt.

But even in that hurt, there
was care.

Because he didn't rush.
Didn't turn away from my wince.

Instead, he kissed my soul,
my cheeks, my lips—

as if to say, **"I
see you."**

"I'm here."
"We're in this together."

His hands were gentle, anchoring my hips,
whispering through touch, **"Breathe,
Shaivi. You're okay."**

And I did.

With every kiss,

I exhaled some fear.

With every press of his palm, I found steadiness in the storm of sensation.

I was unraveling, yes—but not alone.

There was pain, but not abandonment. There was depth, but not danger.

And in the way he moved slower, read my breath, responded to my shifts—I knew:

This wasn't just about desire. It was about being held in the tenderness of being known and being cared for while becoming someone new.

Because pleasure isn't always instant.
Sometimes it rises through the fire of pain,
until trust becomes the balm that makes even
the ache feel worth it.

We paused. Not out of
hesitation—but aware-
ness.

He noticed my shift, my breath catching—
not from pleasure, but from strain.

And instead of pushing through,

he pulled back—not away,
but closer to my comfort.

There's something sacred about a lover who
listens not with ears,

but with hands, with lips, with the
way his eyes ask questions his voice
doesn't need to.

He changed the rhythm. Let go of
what wasn't working, and found
his way to what did.

His hands moved like memory,

like music,

like he wasn't just trying to make me feel good— he was trying to learn me.

And when his fingers explored—
fast, attentive, curious—I felt
known.

Not as a body,
but as a pulse, a
poem, a fire.

I let go of trying to hold back.
Let go of the ache, the doubt,
the past.

Because in that moment, he
wasn't demanding anything.

He was giving.

And my body responded—

not just to the act, but
to the intention.

The care.

The way he stayed.

What we did was raw, yes.

But it was also kind.

Honest.

And sometimes, that's more intimate than anything else.

Endless kisses flowed—
like waves, changing tides,
ever-shifting positions that
spoke of hunger, curiosity,
and quiet longing.

He whispered, *"Come down,"* a
gentle command, an invitation.

But in my chest, a
flutter—not of excitement,
but hesitation.

A breath held tight, a mo-
ment stretched thin.

My eyes searched his— looking
for the safety, the yes, the under-
standing that made my heart slow
instead of race.

I wanted to say yes. Want-
ed to dive in, to give myself
over fully.

But something whispered louder—

I paused— not to stop
the moment, but to hon-
or myself.

To hold space for my
own rhythm. For my
own voice, even when it
trembled.

And in that pause, he
didn't push.

He simply waited, eyes
steady,

breath patient, hands
ready—

not to force, but
to catch.

Because sometimes, the
most powerful *yes* is the
one that comes after the
pause.

He saw the hesitation, and instead
of pressing—he stepped back into
understanding.

No words needed, just a quiet
nod, a softness in his eyes that
said, *"I'm here.*

No rush.
No judgment."

And so,

I chose my own path—
not the one expected, but
the one my heart whis-
pered.

I acclaimed him all— with every kiss, every touch, every breath drawn deep.

My hands spoke what words could not:

"Here.
Now.
This is mine to give."

I traced the lines of his skin, mapped the heat beneath, worshipped the body that held both history and possibility.

Our passion didn't lessen—it changed shape, became a dance of reverence and mutual surrender.

In that sacred exchange, I found power—not in what I did, but in what I chose.

And he met me there—with open arms, with patient fire,

with the quiet knowing that love is not just in acts, but in respect.

He wore the need, etched in the curve of his lips, in the quiet fire behind his eyes— the yearning for more. But I held my ground, soft but firm, whispering truths in a voice only he could hear.

"No worry, no hurry," I said, my breath steady, my heart open. *"Not tonight."*

His smile was patient, understanding, a promise wrapped in silence:

"Whenever you're ready, I'll be here."

There's a grace in knowing when to wait— when to let desire stretch and breathe without pressure.

In that pause, we found trust.

And sometimes, that's the sweetest kind of pleasure.

I had just said, *"No worry, no hurry,"* and I meant it.

But something stirred— not pressure, not obligation, but a quiet kind of courage. A desire to try, to understand, to give in a way that felt like learning someone in the most tender way.

So I moved— slowly, deliberately.

Not to prove anything, but to feel what

it meant to offer myself in this unspoken language.

I watched him unravel, his breath hitch, his body soften into the trust between us.

There was power in my touch, yes— but more than that, there was presence.

And in return, he didn't rush me.
Didn't demand. He
let me lead.

Let me explore.

Let me learn him like a secret I chose to uncover on my own terms.

And in that exchange, in that giving, we found something far more intimate than just the act.

We found belief.

In each other.

In the moment.

In the fragile, fearless way two people choose to meet again—*fully.*

There are moments when time forgets to tick, when breath feels borrowed, and bodies speak louder than thoughts ever could.

He grabbed my hair—gently, but firmly—a
touch between control and reverence.

And I gave. Not just my body, but my trust,
my fire, the softest pieces of myself tucked
beneath the surface for far too long.

I felt breathless—not just from the act, but from the
ache of what it meant to open so fully.

To give all of me.

To hold nothing back.

And yet,

in that dizzying intensity, there
was power.

There was choice.

This wasn't just about pleasure. It was about being
seen, being wanted, being remembered in ways
only two hearts still entangled can feel.

I wasn't silent.
My body spoke.

And he listened.

And in that breathless moment,
I tasted something rare—not just
him, but the wild,

Vulnerable, undeniable truth of my own becoming.

It was quietly rough—not violent, but intense. A push and pull between gentle submission and quiet power.

His breath deepened. Mine, too.

There were no words, just the language of skin and sounds and eyes that locked every now and then just to say, *"I'm still here. I still want you."*

And though my hands trembled

just a little, my
spirit didn't.

Because in that moment, giving wasn't weakness.

It was exploration.

It was boldness wrapped in softness.

After all the ache, all the almosts, all the silences that stretched like sky between us—we met again.

Not in words, but
in skin,

in the hush of breath and the comfort of arms that once knew exactly where I fit.

You beneath me—

a place I once avoided, now a
place I chose.

Not to dominate.

Not to lose myself.

But to feel... everything.

I sat above your heartbeat, felt its thud sync with mine—like two timelines trying to find the same moment again.

Your hands didn't rush. They
read me, like an old letter
rediscovered, creases deep, ink
faded— but meaning still intact.

I didn't close my eyes.
I looked at you.

Because I wanted to remember
how it felt to be seen, to be want-
ed, to be... here.

And in that closeness— our bodies whispered what our mouths never dared:

That this isn't just lust.
This isn't just past. This is something alive, still breathing between us, despite everything.

Even if it ends again, even if goodbye lingers somewhere in the sheets—we had this moment.

And it was ours.

We happened.

Raw.

Unscripted.

The kind of closeness that feels like fire and familiarity, burning through past and present all at once.

It was the best we'd ever been—not because of the way our bodies moved, but because it felt like everything unspoken finally found breath.

— *Shivani Singh*

Eyes Don't Lie

I thought we were one flame, dancing,
daring, undoing all that distance had
built.

Until I saw his eyes.

Not just the lust—
that stayed, burning as
always.
But something underneath.
A flicker.
A shadow.
A truth he didn't speak, but couldn't
hide.

And in that gaze,
I saw questions I wasn't ready to ask, answers I
wasn't sure I wanted to hear.

Was he here entirely, or just physically present, with
pieces of him still tucked away elsewhere?

Was I the echo of something he missed, or the
silence between two mistakes?

His eyes held a storm I couldn't
name.

And mine?

They blinked back all the doubts I tried so hard to bury.

But we didn't speak. We stayed in that warmth, pretending we weren't trembling underneath.

Because even though our bodies were bare, our truths... remained clothed.

Then his body stuttered— like a
song skipping a beat, like a truth
hesitating behind a locked door.

He pulled me close, but
something in him was pulling
away.

His eyes— so good at burning
into me— now

blinked too fast, darted like
they were hiding a name a
thought a guilt that had no
place between us.

Nervousness wrapped around his breath. Not the kind that comes from excitement— but the kind that trembles when you're trying not to be seen too clearly.

And I saw it.

That flicker.

That moment where comfort cracked,
where his ease turned into effort, where his
silence spoke of something he wasn't ready
to say.

And my body, still pressed
against his, went still.

Because in that moment, I knew—
this wasn't just about us. There was
someone else in the room, even if she
wasn't physically there.

And suddenly, the
warmth we built felt
borrowed.

I was right there— on the edge of
surrender, where pleasure wraps around
pain and everything else disappears.

His breath was on my skin, his name
curled inside mine, our bodies spelling
out something we hadn't dared to
write in words.

And yet— somewhere in that
storm,

I felt it.
A silence too calculated, a tremble
that wasn't passion, a presence he
hadn't spoken of, but hadn't quite
let go of either.

My body still ached, but my soul
suddenly didn't.

So I looked at him, smiled
casually, and said—
"I need to go to the washroom."

A sentence so simple.
But beneath it:
a war.
A boundary.
A voice saying,

"Not like this. Not if there's someone else in this space who doesn't belong."

He may have wanted to continue. But I
couldn't.

Because even in love, even
in desire, there has to be
truth.

And if his silence hid *her,* no matter
how much I loved him, I would not

stay in that bed where honesty didn't
lie with us.

I paused.
Because I deserved clarity.
Not closeness built on confusion.

And in that pause, I reclaimed
myself.

I walked away—
naked, not just in
body but in truth.

His touch still lingered on my skin, a memory
not even seconds old. The air

around me hummed with him—
his scent, his heat, his everything.

Inside the washroom, I faced
the mirror.

And for the first time, I saw a version of
me that wasn't waiting for anyone's gaze
to feel beautiful.

I was glowing— not just from
what happened, but from
how I felt *inside* it. My eyes
shimmered.

That smile—
it wasn't playful.
It was sacred.
Like my soul finally let the light come through.

I stood there, still,
breathing.
Knowing this was mine— this glow,
this feeling.

But also knowing...

Something would change when I
walked back out.

It was just instinct. That quiet gut
feeling that dances right before the air
turns.

And yet, I didn't flinch.
I didn't rush. I took one
last look,
held onto that light, because no matter what waited
beyond that door— **this version of me was real.**

And nothing could take that away.

I stepped out— bare, but not broken. Still glowing,
still wrapped in everything we had just become.

And without a word, I leaned into
him. From head to toe, kiss after kiss,
smooches carrying
more than lust— they carried care, clarity,
and something unspoken
I wasn't yet ready to ask.

My head found its way to his chest,
where his heartbeat lived. That place
where truth hides between ribs and
breath.

I rested there— not to listen for answers, but
just to feel his warmth one more time.

Because even in doubt, even in
silence,

even in all the things he hadn't said— he still felt
like home.

And maybe I was foolish. Or
maybe I was brave. But in
that moment,
I wasn't choosing to question. I was
choosing to be.

To exist in the hush between pleasure
and pain, between knowing and not
knowing.

Because love isn't always loud. Sometimes, it's just a body leaning into another hoping that this closeness still means the same.

His voice broke the silence, soft but
sharp—
"Shaivi, I am feeling bad for her."
The girl he chose after me. The
girl who was once my closest
friend.

And just like that— our
moment became his betrayal.

The room froze, the
warmth drained,
and all that was
tender twisted into
something jagged.

His words hung between us— a
shadow I hadn't invited, a crack in
the glow.

That moment, the fire between us
flickered— not from lack of desire,
but from the weight of betrayal,
the heavy hand of guilt.

I felt it, the invisible line we had crossed,
the secret we weren't ready to name.

And yet,

in the silence that followed,
I asked myself—
Was this love from his side?
Or just the echo of something lost?

My head still resting against his steady chest, his fingers tracing the map of my skin— soft, tender, like he's memorizing me.

And then his words— whispered,
heavy— falling into the space
between us:

**"I want to marry her. She
is my everything."** as if I
hadn't just given him all of
me.

The warmth of his touch collides with the chill of what he's just said. A truth that wraps around my heart like a thorny vine.

How can love feel so close,
yet be so far away? His hands,

gentle and sure, but his heart
speaking a different language.

I stayed still—a quiet storm raging
inside me, trying to hold on to the
fragments of what we shared, even
as his words pulled the ground from
beneath.

Because sometimes love is not enough—not when it's tangled with promises made to another.

I had no words—not because
I didn't feel, but because some
truths are too fragile to speak
aloud.

In the heavy air between us, I
chose silence—a quiet offering,
a soft shelter for his storm.

He had to leave—to ride out to Madhav's
place, while my heart wrestled with the
weight of what he said, and what we both
held inside.

I became the silent witness—letting
him speak his truth, letting the
tension breathe, holding the space
between us without breaking it.

I swallowed every word, every
ache, every scream—not because
I forgave, but because I cared
enough to keep him safe.

I didn't speak. Not
then. Because I
didn't want my
heartbreak

to ride with him on his bike, into an
accident of conscience.

Even when the truth cut deep, even
when betrayal burned, I chose love
that whispers through restraint,
that protects from afar.

Because sometimes the strongest
thing we can do is hold back the
storm—and hope the silence
holds us both until we can
breathe again.

— *Shivani Singh*

Departure

He got dressed. I did
too.

Awkward now.

All that once felt familiar, now
heavy with the silence we dared
not break.

Distance creeping in where warmth
had just been.

The moment stretched— a
fragile thread holding us just
before goodbye.

And in that pause, I caught the
glimpse of a man torn between
what he wanted and what he had
to face.

The night stretched long,
quiet between us— minutes
passing like shadows, heavy and
unspoken.

I kept distance— while on the bike—on the way to my friend's place, a silent shield against what lingered in the air.

Until suddenly— he loosened the clutch and reached for my hand.

Held it.
Like a lover.
Like nothing had changed.

But everything had.

Warmth seeped through the cold, a quiet promise in his grip: **"I'm here. I see you."**

Words left unsaid folded into that touch, as the bike hummed beneath us, and the city lights blurred around our silent journey.

He held on through the miles and the night— a tether between what was, what is, and what might never be.

EVEN IF I BREAK, TRUTH MUST STAND

What he did was wrong— to me, and to Disha, the one he was with. I couldn't process it— not then. She deserved the truth, no matter what she'd done. Even when betrayal came from her hand, once my closest friend— almost a sister, even when she chose to break us, not bend. Her betrayal was sharp— a blade to my chest, worse than silence, worse than the rest. She knew I love him, yet walked that line, and still— I cannot unlove him, not today, not anytime. Maybe not even till my final breath,

that ache, that
quiet death.

But she—

she does not deserve this lie.
Not the cheating, not the why.
She left so much for him—
friends, and me. Even cried for
me once, silently. Once, she
made me better. Once, she lit
my way. And somewhere in my
heart, that gratitude still stays.
She is a girl— a soul, in herself,
an entire world And betrayal,
I believe, can never stay curled.

It unravels— truth finds a
door. If he's done it now, he'll
do it more.

That's the cruelest thing he could ever do, to
someone who gave up so much, she tried to
make it look true. I can't control his choices,
but I can choose mine.

Silence would make me guilty by design.

How will she feel when the
truth is clear— that I was
the one, and he was near?
She might hate me, but at
least she'll know. He may
twist it all, but truth will
still show. He might beg
her to stay, cloak his guilt
in charm, pretend it was
nothing, do more harm.
But I decided— not in
that moment, but the one
next— to tell her.

Not for revenge, not out of
rage— but because I must live
with my own page. And then
came the thought— of death,
of fate. A test, a whisper, a
shadow too late.

What if cancer grows in me unseen?

What if my life slips in between?

That's why, from day one, I
never asked him to stay— just
watched him,

loved him, and walked away.
Another thought struck—
should I let it all be? Let her
have him, at least care for him,
not me? I grew selfish for a
single breath. But what about
her? What about theft—

of truth, of right, of something
beneath the core? She too deserves
love that's honest and sure. So
I decided, in quiet resolve— I
would try to make him evolve.

To confess, to stand in light, to not
let her sleep beside a lie each night.
Because even if my voice breaks, it
will still be true. That's the kind of
love She deserves too.

I said bye— not knowing if this was
forever, or just a pause in a story still
aching to be told.

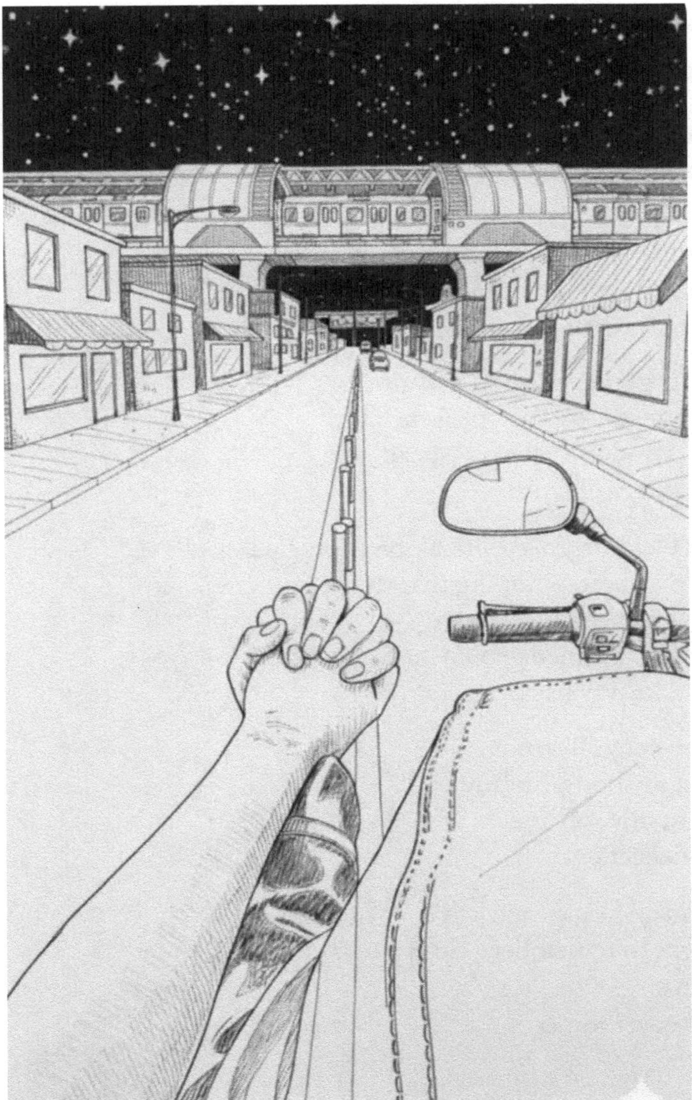

Before the night, I
loved him— whole and
unguarded— gave my
all, wrapped in trust like a
fragile thread.

He held me in that moment,
and I believed— that love
was enough, that loyalty was
spoken without words.

But goodbyes don't wait for
promises to be proven, and
hearts don't always speak the
language of truth.

So I let him go— with a prayer tangled
in my chest— hoping that the love I
gave was real,
and that someday, somehow, it might
find its way back.

I gave my all— not
just my body, but my
trust, my softness,
my belief.

And all he gave me was a
night to remember— and a
truth
I'll never forget.

— *Shivani Singh*

At Her Doorstep

He stopped the bike, hands unsure, eyes asking questions he wouldn't say— *Does she know?*

Did you tell her what we did today?

I said no— since he didn't want her to know, I'd keep our secret safe.

Down came Vanditi, puzzled and late, a question in her walk, a smirk on her lips— **"Bro, payment done?"** she joked, thinking he was just a ride.

He played along, eyes still fixed on me, and I, lips curled in a quiet yes— a shared lie between glances.

Inside, shoes off, truth began
to tug.

"Who was he?" "Uber," I
muttered, but lies don't sit well
with her.
"Tell me everything," she said.
So I did.
Rudra Trivedi —
She mentioned the one you love, the one
who didn't care.

Shock washed her face, then teasing—
"Something sinful?" I nodded,
blushing like the sky before a storm.

"You two can't even stand each other,"
she said, half-laughing, **"and
now this?"** broken rules,
tangled hearts

But she saw it— my glow, heart pounding, a
new ache blooming wild, the love in my silence,
bleeding the secret of first love, the tender sting
of innocence lost, the heavy weight of desire. and
something more.

My legs hurt.
There was spotting. I bled a
moment I didn't know would hurt
this much— or mean this much.

And then the music curled around the room—
slow, smoky, aching—

"Jal raha hoon, ab bujh jaane ko dil karta hai..." It wasn't just background. It was our soundtrack. Every note flickered with the fire we'd just lit between us. And I, still burning, felt it wrap me like his breath once did— too close, too deep.

"Teri zulfon mein ulajh jaane ko dil karta hai..." Yes.
I had been tangled.
In his eyes, in his hands, in that
moment that had no name, but left
a mark all the same.

"Dil karta hai, tujhe kar loon main qareeb itna..." I had
been that close.
Close enough to feel the weight of want
pressed into my skin, and still echoing in my
bones.

"Ke teri saanson mein ab ghul jaane ko dil karta Hai" I
didn't just hear that line— I had lived it.
Moments ago.
Before I stepped into this room, before blue
lights and questions.

And now, the song remembered
what I was still trying to hold.

...And then the song turned, whispered what I had
hoped to hear from him—

"Dil de vich de-de thodi jehi thaan tu..." Just a little space in your heart.
That's all I ever wanted.
Not a label, not a future—just space.
A little place where I wasn't a mistake.

"Naa de peeche Laa le mera naa tu..."
Attach my name behind your name—
Let me be part of your story, Not a shadow you hide away. But he didn't

Not with words. Not with action.

He left before naming what we were— what we could've been.

And yet—
his eyes lingered too long, his silence felt too loud, his face... told me what his mouth never dared.

That he cared.
That maybe, in another world, he would've stayed.

But in this one— he didn't.

Blue lights flickered softly, momos steamed in the quiet room, and I held fragile hope in

trembling hands, pads pressed close to skin
that still hurt.

"Did you use protection?" Her voice
sharp— a slap of reality— **"You're
doing grown-up things but acting
like children."** Disappointed but
caring, she wrapped me in kindness.

"Where did he go?"
I whispered,
"To meet his friends."
And in that quiet, I held
the weight of love, pain,
and secrets still untold.

— *Shivani Singh*

The Morning After

You messaged me as day began,
"Are you okay, Shaivi? Just tell me if you can." I
replied with a steady, quiet tone, *"Yes, I'm fine, not*
all alone.
There was some bleeding, just a trace— *It's normal*
after... that first embrace."

You paused, your words a gentle plea,
"Bleeding?" you asked so worriedly. I
softened it with calm, precise, *"It's*
something natural, nothing twice. Just
biology, it's understood— It happens,
and it's all good."

"So... virginity?" you asked in doubt, I
nodded softly, spelling it out. *"No, it's*
gone," I said with grace, The truth lay
quiet in that space.

You sent an emoji, broken, scared, *"We shouldn't have,"* you gently shared.

"It's just a hymen, nothing more,
A tear that's known in myth and lore."*
But you replied, your heart off-track,
"Don't give me science—I'm breaking back!"

"I know," I said, *"don't lose your peace,* There's nothing wrong, please let it cease.

And if I need you, I will say,
For now, I'm truly okay today."*

I shifted tones, tried to be light,
"We made momos late last night."
You asked me, *"Did your friends all know?"*
"No," I said, *"I let it go."*

"One asked in front of you, remember?
She thought we rode with a Rapido member."* You chuckled then, a laugh released, But still your mind had not found peace.

"Just don't overthink," I said with care, *"Take time, breathe slow, be more aware."* You asked again, *"Are you truly alright?" "Yes,"* I said, *"I've told you no lie."*

"You're in my diary now," you shared,
"A part of thoughts I've never aired."
I teased, *"You said you don't write anymore."*
"Now the words just live in my core."

"Please," I begged, *"no deathly talk,*
No 'after I'm gone' poetic walk."* You
sighed, *"I meant you're now a part Of secrets*
buried deep in heart."

"Okay," I said, *"but write them clear,*
Your riddles fill the heart with fear."*

You whispered, *"I'm on a regretful ride,* A trip I
never meant to hide."*

I said, *"You love trips, but not this lane. Regret should not*
become your chain."

You asked,
"But how do I not go?

You lost it... To someone
like me.

Someone selfish.
Someone who doesn't care like he should."*

I smiled through ache and let you speak, Your
words, your shame, your spirit weak. *"You sound*

like memes that claim their right, 'My life, my rules,'
despite the fight.

But what you think is not always real,
The truth can hide, the truth can heal."*

You said, *"I know what comes from here—* Guilt will
grow and draw me near.

Then I'll stop talking, pull away,
And soon enough we'll drift, decay."*

I whispered, *"Let your feelings flow,*
But give yourself some time to grow."* You
sighed, *"I'll sleep on time instead."* I warned,
"Guilt will haunt your head." Then softly, truth
came breaking free— *"Shaivi, I love Disha...*
deeply.

More than anything I've ever known, I never
meant to hurt you or own.

You are the kindest soul I've met,
And hurting you—I will regret."*

I held it with a quiet smile,
"Some things just happen... stay awhile.
They're meant to be, though unclear how,
But we're both breathing through it now."*

You sent a hug, through words, through air,
"Take care of you. You're rare, so rare."

I said, *"And you love her—hold it close.*
Choose what's right for you both the most."*
You ended soft with truth and grace,
"She owns my life, my every space."

"And I replied— Not with a
scream,

Not with a plea, or a shattered dream.
Just one word, tossed like a stone in a pool—
"Cool."

But oh, what a storm that silence hid,
Behind that word, behind that lid.
Not apathy, no peace, no rule— Just
trembling fingers typing cool.

A dam disguised in four small letters, A flood of
"what ifs," bitter, unfettered.

A thousand thoughts I'll never school, Drowned in one...
"Cool."

But let me tell you what that word really meant:

Cool— Was A
mask.
A straight spine in a collapsing heart.

Cool—
Was a laugh choking on its own silence.
A fist clenched around
Everything I wouldn't say.

Cool—
Was four letters that said: *"Don't*
worry, I'll bleed in private." So
yeah... *Cool.*

That's what I gave him. Because saying
"You broke me"

Would've been far too warm.

— *Shivani Singh*

ABOUT THE AUTHOR

Shivani Singh's writing journey began in 2019 after hearing the motivational rapper Abhinav Prateek (Abby Viral). The initial scattered notes on strength and social change soon blossomed into a singular focus: love.

Her poetry maps the evolution of a young woman through desire, ache, faith, and divine connection. She writes love the way it is lived—raw, spiritual, and overwhelmingly real. Shivani doesn't dilute or decorate; her voice is unfiltered and explicit, capturing the deeply human experience of romance, spirituality, and feminine truth.

Her lines feel like a soul remembering itself—a voice both young and ancient in its knowing, tender yet unafraid, deeply rooted.

This debut book is not merely a collection of poems—it is a sanctuary. A quiet, luminous space for those who have loved beyond logic, who have broken open instead of breaking down, who have loved deeply, or found themselves awakening to a tenderness they cannot explain.

Through her work, she invites readers into the quiet corners of the heart where longing, healing, and truth coexist.